The Marching

BAND NERDS

Handbook

Rules from **The 13th Chair** Trombone Player

Written By
DJ Corchin

Illustrated By
Dan Dougherty

The phazelFOZ Company, LLC

THE MARCHING BAND NERDS HANDBOOK
Copyright © 2012 By DJ Corchin

Published by The phazelFOZ Company, LLC.
Chicago, Illinois
www.phazelfoz.com

Library of Congress Number 2012907527

ISBN   978-0-9834876-7-8 (Hardcover)
       978-0-9819645-7-7 (Paperback)
       978-0-9834876-6-1 (eBook)

The
13th
Chair

"Joining us"... from The 13th Chair Trombone Player, a fun and insightful look at the crazy world of Marching Band! DJ Corchin has done it again. Through his "rules" DJ, takes the activity we love and shows us measure by measure why we love it. I declare The Marching Band Nerds Handbook to be required reading for all incoming band Freshman. (Also Seniors, Parents, Directors, Administrators and... well, you get where I'm going here...) Go for it... Break Ranks!"

Chuck Henson
The "Voice" of Bands of America

"DJ has done it again! He has mixed wit and wisdom into a trek through band memories. If you have been a part of a marching band family, you will have faces from your past to match these pages. If you have not been a part of marching band yet, you may see a bit of the future. Enjoy and laugh. Remember. (Or prepare!) Be sure to take the time to see the many valuable lessons, too."

Greg Bimm
Director of Bands
Marian Catholic High School, Chicago Heights, IL

"DJ Corchin is good medicine. His ability to examine the marching world from a slightly different angle delivers a healthy dose of equal parts humor and inspiration. The Marching Band Nerds Handbook is a perfect prescription that is sure to keep band students, directors, and parents in step."

Ken Martinson
Founder of Marching.com

"DJ does it again! Band nerds of all ages will enjoy the humorous, thoughtful, and clever lessons presented in the book. Witty illustrations by Dan Dougherty add an extra level of value."

Courtney Brandt
Author of The Line Series and
Confessions of a Teenage Band Geek

"DJ has such a unique way of looking at what we do every day in band class and on the marching field. As band directors, we not only teach the first chair students, we (at least) try to teach and inspire every student in every chair. The lessons and the laughs in this book will help many band directors keep their feet in time and their humor in check."

Ben Harloff
Original Blast Cast: Trumpet Soloist
Carolina Crown Brass Staff

"DJ has done it again with his great insight into the everyday lives of all of us Band Nerds. He has the unique ability to take a new, jovial look at the situations we took for granted, the behaviors we ignored, and the personalities we had forgotten about after years of therapy. If only I had this book and these rules while coming up through the ranks, I'm sure that I would have have had at least a few less awkward moments."

Jeff Handel
Associate Director of Bands and Percussion
Wando High School, Mount Pleasant , SC

"Oh my...still laughing! I literally wanted to tear every other page out and plaster it on my colleagues' lockers or make it into a t-shirt. Some things about band never change."

Amy McCabe
Trumpet/Cornetist;
"The President's Own" United States Marine Band

Dedicated to

T.S.

From the outside looking in, no one understands it.
From the inside looking out, no one can explain it.

Fun

Fun is the greatest luxury of our time. It's become our way of rewarding ourselves after the real "important things" are taken care of. Having fun, although we like to say it's important, is extremely underrated. Fun should be the supercharged, nuclear, cosmic fuel that can power the world towards the way we always hoped it to be. If more people were having fun, there would be no reason for hate or discrimination or any other evil. Regardless of your world and social views the truth remains: Evil is not fun, Good is fun. Fun is inclusive, loving, humorous, healing, and everything else that moves us forward. To all the people who are slowing us down...lighten up. Grab a cupcake and chill out. The world's lost a bit of its will to have fun. To me, that's dumb. I don't want to be dumb.

Treat others how you want to be treated.

It's a salute, not interpretive dance.

Every day is a deodorant day.

Never put a freshman on water duty.

Never put a senior on water duty.

**"Dress Right" has two meanings.
Both equally important.**

Band parents mean well.

Passion is good.

Compassion is better.

Don't lock your knees when standing at attention.

Revenge is sweet.

Careful what you post online.

Don't let the guard lead stretches.

Technology can enhance the show...

...except in the rain.

Trombone slides are not lightsabers.

**Don't worry about what's going on
in the back of the bus.
It's better you don't know.**

**Live animals are not a
good idea for any show.**

Trumpets...calm down.

**Being in charge of the metronome
ain't so bad.**

When life seems too big to overcome,
slow it down, take one measure at a time,
and subdivide.

Band Nerds

"Pay-Attention-To-Us-At-A-Football-Game" Kit

1. Fog Horn
2. Six foot gigantic trophy w/movable cart
3. Bikinis for the band
   ...EVERYONE in the band.
4. T-Shirt rocket launcher
5. Hometown reality pop star
6. Emergency Earth, Wind, & Fire music
7. A backbeat
8. A backflip to a backbeat while back'n that thang up
9. 8 gigantic drums in the front
10. A cute puppy

**Never give drummers metal sticks.
They think they're ninjas.**

But most ninjas are clarinet players.

Band parents *are* adults.
But that doesn't mean they don't
need supervision.

**What happens in sectionals,
stays in sectionals.**

Don't be "that person" during the company front.

No energy drinks before the show.

Although you must focus on where you're going, don't forget about what you're doing.

If you get a flute solo...rock it.

There's something to be said for being a nerd.

Seriously...no more fire out of the tuba bell.

Toes up...

...'cause ya never know.

Pyramids don't work in marching band.

Use a special mellophone mouthpiece when possible. It makes it easier to stay on your face.

Let the uniform parents do their job.
They probably know best.

Never try to make a French Horn shaped formation. It's just too confusing.

**Law of the jungle:
Serve or be served.**

Directors can wear t-shirts and shorts during rehearsals.

Never run with a piccolo.

Always run with a sousaphone.

**Be nice to alternates.
You never know when they'll
be your drum major.**

Earn respect. Don't demand it.

Marching Band is an art not a sport.

But if it were a sport, the drummers would win.

Make sure to respect your elders.

They need it in today's day and age.

**Don't expect too much from saxes
during a horn flash.**

Don't expect <u>anything</u> from baritones.

Use the force.

It's easier on the back.

Practice 8 to 5 whenever you can.

But not 24 to 5.

There is such a thing as "over performing."

**As cool as gauntlets are,
they should only be worn during
band performances.**

Invest in a full length mirror.

Take what you do seriously.

But don't take yourself too seriously.

**Always make sure the bari sax player
is taller than the instrument.**

Give the announcer the phonetic spellings.

68

There's a reason bassoons don't march.

If you make a mistake...sell it.

Don't cut the band's funding.

It's not a pretty sight.

Wear the right color socks.

Cheese fundraisers are not a good idea in the summer.

Beauty is in the eye of the beholder.

A real piano is too much for band parents.

Don't take "pit" literally.

**Clarinets,
Don't worry. Someone, somewhere,
hears you.**

Having the band dance is cool.

Just don't forget about your instruments.

**Angels don't have a favorite instrument.
They love everyone.**

Never serve sushi before a competition.

Flutes,
Be sure to work out your
left shoulder too.

Some things aren't meant to be tossed.

**Hockey and band DO have
something in common.**

Listen to your section leader.
Your life may depend on it.

Bring a bigger blanket.

**Be sure to think about any
pass-throughs before running the drill.**

The performance is a celebration of all your hard work, not the culmination of it.

Don't use rubber sticks.

Balloons are not a good idea.

Go to the bathroom BEFORE practice.

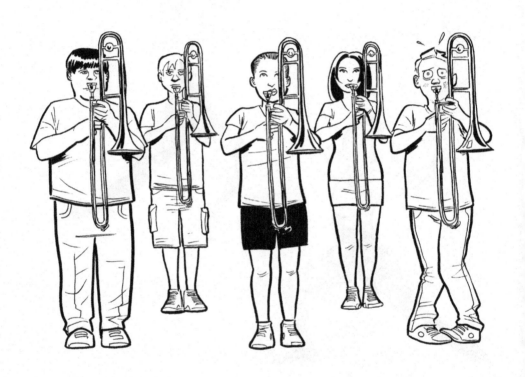

On your first day, ask more questions instead of knowing all the answers.

Make sure people can understand your show.

Size doesn't matter...much.

**If a judge gets in your way,
keep marching.**

Just make sure it's not right before a halt.

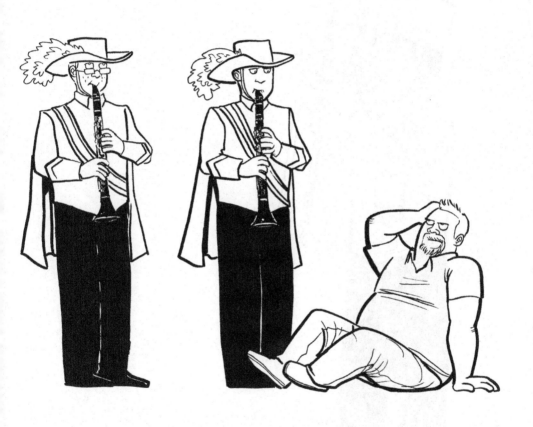

Never lick your horn before a cold night performance.

**Actually, never lick your horn.
That's just weird.**

**Teach the parents the appropriate
time to applaud.**

**Stay hydrated.
Rehearsal in the heat is hot.**

Color guard's famous last words, "Trust Me."

Make sure to mic the oboe solo.
They just can't handle fortissimo.

Don't judge a book by its cover.

Judge it by its spine.

Stick to the basics at the concession stand.

If it's windy, don't toss.

Sometimes props can be too much.

Don't fight amongst ourselves.

**When designing the guard costumes,
keep in mind the month of November.**

It's a podium,
not a studio apartment.

Never use Velcro shoes.

Don't forget to turn off the mic.

**Only fart during the loud parts.
That's what the f stands for.**

That includes the audience.

The Unscalable Wall

My marching band and I reached an unscalable wall.
We tried to climb over but it's impossibly tall.
It's a million feet wide, and a billion yards up.
We tried to march through it but that wasn't enough.

There were words on the wall that were scattered about.
Words like difficult, impossible, fear, and self doubt.
Sometimes we'd feel like we wanted to quit.
That the wall was much bigger than we'd like to admit.

But we'd pick ourselves up, and break down our parts.
We'd drill in our moves 'till we knew them by heart.
The judges would judge us show after show,
The wall's shadow upon us wherever we'd go.

But when Finals arrived the words were not taunting.
The wall was still there but it wasn't as daunting.
In the end it was us that the audience crowned.
We made a wall of our own, a wall of our sound.

Have fun.

Peace with a whole lotta hair grease.

See ya.

- The 13th Chair

A special Band Nerds thank you to:

Jessica
Mom
Scott
Chance
Meg
Kevin
Greg Bimm
Courtney Brandt
Ben Harloff
Chuck Henson
Jeff Handel
Ken Martinson
Amy McCabe
Jason Wick

Also check out...

BAND NERDS

Poetry From The 13th Chair Trombone Player

The
13th
Chair

www.the13thchair.com

CPSIA information can be obtained
at www.ICGtesting.com
Printed in the USA
BVOW03s1133131117
500061BV00005B/58/P